GLASS
in
Colonial Williamsburg's
Archaeological
Collections

GLASS

in

Colonial Williamsburg's Archaeological Collections

by

IVOR NOËL HUME

Published by
The COLONIAL WILLIAMSBURG FOUNDATION
Williamsburg, Virginia

ISBN 0-910412-06-5

LC No. 79-84022

SECOND PRINTING, 1976

Printed in the United States of America

ACKNOWLEDGEMENTS

Colonial Williamsburg is indebted to the Smithsonian Institution for permission to illustrate items from its Clay Bank and Tutter's Neck collections, and to Mr. L. B. Weber of Newport News for the use of an example from Denbigh Plantation.

PREFACE

Although most of the glass illustrated in this booklet was found in archaeological excavations, it is hoped that it will be of interest and value not only to archaeologists but also to collectors.

The dating of glass used in colonial America is often extremely difficult, for very few of the surviving pieces have dates actually engraved or molded on them. Many of the examples illustrated here, however, were recovered from sealed archaeological contexts that enable us to determine the approximate dates after which they were thrown away. While these dates do not necessarily coincide with those of the items' manufacture, the archaeological evidence provides important new information about the kinds of glassware that were in use in individual households at specific moments in history.

All the photographed examples were excavated in Williamsburg and its vicinity or relate to pieces that were found here; unless otherwise stated, all are in the archaeological collections of Colonial Williamsburg. For the benefit of those who may desire to cite the illustrated specimens in their own archaeological reports, or who wish to compare them with glass in other collections, the catalog number and measurements of each item are listed on pages 46–48.

I.N.H.

December 1968.

FIGURE 1
A group of wine glasses found in a well at the Williamsburg home site of John Custis, probably thrown away on instructions from Martha Dandridge Custis Washington. The glasses range in date from about 1695 to 1725.

I n the heat of an August day in 1653 a team of four appraisers walked through the home of the late Captain Stephen Gill carefully recording and valuing its contents in terms of tobacco. In one room they found:

> 1 Small side Table and striped Carpett, 1 Small Pewter Sifterine and Bason and a Bason stoole. 1 Livery Cubbard with Glasses and Earthenware upon it.

The appraisers would have been hard put to value each glass and pot separately when one pound of tobacco was the smallest unit of value, so they thought awhile and wrote down the table, carpet, cupboard, and the rest as being worth two hundred pounds all together. We shall never know how many glasses were counted or whether they were cheap cigar-stemmed drinking glasses from London or elaborate dragonesque creations from Venice. We know only that glass was arrayed on the livery cupboard and so was probably thought ornamental as well as useful. Such had been the dual role played by glass from the days of ancient Egypt to the present, although its contributions to beauty have been as varied as the concepts of beauty itself.

When James I sat on the English throne and the first colonists were hacking holes in the Jamestown wilderness, the Englishman's glass was subject to two major foreign influences, from Lorraine and Venice. The former laid its stress on utility—beakers, bottles, phials, lamps, window glass—and the latter on elegance in both form and color. Venetian drinking glasses were then the mark of a man of substance, and in Virginia the presence of such opulence was cause for a diarist's comment. On March 11, 1633, the Dutch traveler David Pietersz reached Jamestown where he was greeted by Governor Harvey who then "proceeded with me to his house, where he bid me welcome with a Venice glass of sack."

The term Venice glass referred as much to the vessel's elegant style as to its place of manufacture, for similar shapes and decorative techniques were employed both in the Netherlands and in England, the products in both cases being described as *à la façon de Venise*. The soda lime metal[1] was both light and thin, and in England lacked the crystal-sharp brilliance of the better European products. The majority of examples recovered from early colonial contexts in Virginia are not of the best—but neither are most of those of similar date from English excavations.

No early seventeenth-century glass has been recovered from Williamsburg excavations, and one is tempted to conclude that its absence is evidence of its fragility and inability to survive in use for any extended length of time. However, ceramics of the first half of the century are also absent, while examples from even the last years of the seventeenth century are of extreme rarity. It must therefore be concluded that few colonists settling in Williamsburg brought their old pottery or glass with them. Nevertheless, the evolution of glass through the seventeenth century cannot be summarily dismissed from any account of what has been found in Williamsburg, for the passage of the old affected the emergence of the new.

---

1. The term *metal* is used to describe the vitreous material, while *glass* is reserved to define the products: drinking glass, wine glass, looking glass, etc.

The two abortive glassmaking ventures near Jamestown in 1608 and 1621 have no bearing on the story and are of interest here only in that those enterprises, and their two sets of artificers, represented both avenues of glass development, the first being manned by German makers of green "forest" glass or *Waldglas* and the second by a team of Italians who were presumably expecting to produce clear drinking glasses *à la façon de Venise*. Another glassmaking operation is believed to have been launched at Governor Berkeley's Green Spring plantation in the mid-seventeenth century, but the site has not been fully explored and the evidence so far forthcoming reveals only that a green metal comparable to that used in bottlemaking was melted there. Here ends the history of colonial glassmaking in Virginia—with the exception of an attempt in 1766 by merchant John Mercer to establish a bottle factory. He advertised in the *Virginia Gazette* for April 18, 1766, saying that he would set up the factory if he received sufficient encouragement. But presumably he did not, for no further announcements survive and no evidence of glassmaking was found when his plantation at Marlborough in Stafford County was excavated in 1956.

The history of glassmaking in England from the late sixteenth to the end of the seventeenth century is one of monopolies and embargoes, the monopolies controlling the distribution of both talent and profits, and the embargoes protecting the monopolists. The principal effect of the latter was to minimize the flow of fine Venetian glassware into England, particularly in the first half of the seventeenth century. Although glassmaking had been going on in southeastern England since the thirteenth century, not until the sixteenth century did the manufacturers venture far into the field of table glass. Venetian workmen were brought to London to produce *cristallo* drinking glasses in 1571. However, the first major step in this direction came with the arrival of a Venetian, Giacomo Verzelini, who in 1575 received a royal license giving him the sole right to produce Venice glass in England. Surviving examples are of majestic quality and are embellished with diamond point engraving probably executed by a Frenchman named Anthony de Lysle.

Verzelini retired in 1592, and during the next thirty years the English glassmaking industry passed through the hands of various rather ineffectual licensees until Sir Robert Mansell obtained a grant of letters patent in 1623. This gave him the sole right to:

> practise sett up and putt into use the arte feate and misterie
> of melting and makeing of all manner of drinking glasses broade
> glasses windowe glasses looking glasses and all other kinds of
> glasses, bugles bottles violls or vessels whatsoever made of glass
> of any fashion stuff matter or metal whatsoever . . .

From this monopoly document nothing was omitted save punctuation. With it in hand, Mansell set about establishing a nationwide glass industry, existing factories being regimented into an overall scheme so that the products were diversified to produce what was required, when and where it was needed. Mirror-plate making was developed at Lambeth, window glass was produced at Newcastle, bottles in Southwark, and drinking glasses were made by Venetians and Mantuans at Mansell's Broad Street works in London. The monopoly remained absolute until the Civil War (1642–1649), but by the end of it Mansell was old and the Puritanism of the Commonwealth was having an adverse effect on the sale of elegant drinking glasses. Consequently the Mansell monopoly was allowed to lapse.

Fragments of Mansell-type glasses have been found at Jamestown, although not in large numbers. Much more plentiful are pieces of the styles popular in the years following the restoration of the monarchy in 1660. Our principal source of information regarding the new shapes is derived from the correspondence between two London glass sellers, Michael Measey and John Greene, and their Venetian manufacturer, Allesio Morelli. These letters, now in the British Museum, date between 1667 and 1673 and are illustrated with a vast number of designs, styles that are frequently encountered on archaeological sites of the period 1670–1685.

Even after they were gone, the sobering influence of Oliver Cromwell and his Roundheads may have played a part in the development of taste in English glass. The delicate elegance so characteristic of Venetian style glasses before the Civil War was not revived; in its stead came sturdier glasses whose bowls rather than stems were their dominant features. Made in as few as three parts (bowl, stem-knop, and foot) the new drinking glasses were much more stable than were those of

Verzelini's day when stems were sometimes made from five or six components. The metal, too, had changed, and being thicker was described as *Christall de roache,* rock crystal, instead of the all-encompassing *cristallo* of earlier years.

With the return of King Charles II, new patents were granted, principally to George Villiers, duke of Buckingham, who half-heartedly promoted experiments and researches into the creation of a better metal. Much more vigorous was the encouragement provided by the newly incorporated Worshipful Company of Glass Sellers whose simple object was to promote the manufacture of products that the public would buy—and the public wanted glass that was bright, clear, and strong. The company tried to import it from Venice but found that to maintain standards they had to control manufacture. This frustrating, long-distance operation convinced them that they were better employed trying to improve the home-blown English metals, a goal that could best be reached by setting up their own factory.

In 1674 the glass sellers entered into an agreement with George Ravenscroft, a London merchant with an interest in glass chemistry, who had built a glasshouse at the Savoy in London and who was then applying for a patent to manufacture a new kind of "Christalline glass." The agreement cornered the whole of Ravenscroft's output and authorized him to set up another glasshouse outside London where he could continue experiments to produce an even better metal. Ravenscroft's "Christalline glass" had been subject to a crazing or "crizzling" of the surface that rather resembled the skeleton of a leaf and thus badly marred the clarity of the products. In experimenting to overcome this problem Ravenscroft altered the proportions of salts used in his mix and added small quantities of lead oxide. Late in 1675 he revealed the results to his delighted sponsors who subsequently issued a certificate declaring that the crizzling problem had been solved. In October 1676 the glass sellers decreed that their new flint glasses should be marked with a seal to deter copiers, and the next year they agreed that this should take the form of a raven's head, the rebus of George Ravenscroft.

Examples of glass marked with the glass sellers' seal have been found at Jamestown and there is little doubt that these were manufactured before Ravenscroft's death in 1681. However, they are not of spectacular quality, and it is known that even after the seal was in use some of Ravenscroft's glass continued to suffer from crizzling. After his death the Savoy glasshouse was operated by his erstwhile partner, Hawley Bishopp, under whom the glass sellers' glasses continued to be produced. The monopoly was not maintained, and other London glassmakers were quick to produce similar flint glass while continuing experiments involving the addition of increasing quantities of lead oxide. In consequence, the metal became heavier and more brilliant, and designs were developed to take advantage of those characteristics.

The finest example of the immediately post-Ravenscroft lead glass yet unearthed in America was found by Williamsburg archaeologists investigating a small house site at Clay Bank in Gloucester County (*Figure 2*). Unfortunately only the stem survives, and it is debatable whether it supported a candlestick or a large, lidded goblet *(Figure 2a)*.

FIGURE 2
A seemingly unique stem from either a goblet or a candlestick. This magnificent example of English lead glass dates from about 1685 and was found in a cellar hole at Clay Bank in Gloucester County.

FIGURE 2a
The Clay Bank stem reconstructed both as a candlestick and a goblet.

FIGURE 2   FIGURE 2a

The latter is more probable, although it is surprising that such a splendid object should have found its way to so unimportant a home site. Although goblets with lids were most likely to be found in the great houses of the English aristocracy, there is evidence that they were also to be seen in Virginia. In 1732 Thomas Jones of Williamsburg made a settlement upon his wife in case of his demise, listing among the chattels "6 glass decanters, 6 glasses with covers."

The earliest drinking glasses found in Williamsburg date from the last years of the seventeenth century, a fact that is not surprising when one recalls that little existed there before the city was founded in 1699. The oldest of these glasses *(Figure 3 right)* have small quatrefoil stems and may well have been made during Hawley Bishopp's management of the Savoy glasshouse. However, these are few and far between; the majority of the early examples have heavy, and largely solid, baluster stems. Such glasses are notable for their pleasing composition of mass

FIGURE 3
Three of the earliest drinking-glass stems from Williamsburg excavations. Left: Ale glass with a winged stem below a collar, the wings decorated with hatching from the tongs that pinched them out; about 1685–1695. Center: Goblet with hollow, truncated cone stem, and a broad rib-molded round funnel bowl, the metal a pale green, perhaps a product of an English country factory; about 1680–1690. Right: Goblet or wine glass, the stem a truncated cone pinched into quatrefoil shape; about 1685–1700.

FIGURE 4
Early baluster and related wine glass stems: (1) inverted baluster; about 1690–1705. (2) inverted baluster over a knop; about 1695–1720. (3) drop knop with knops proper above and below; about 1700–1710. (4) expanded angular stem over a knop; about 1700–1720. (5) inverted baluster below a large annulated knop; about 1705–1720. All with tears except No. 2; Nos. 4 and 5 with additional tears in their bowl bases.

rather than for their delicacy of line. By 1690 the sense of weight was being reduced by the insertion of air bubbles into both stems and heavy bowl bases, a device serving both to lighten and to increase refraction *(Figure 4)*.

The first thirty years of the eighteenth century were devoted largely to the development of shapes, and the simple baluster and inverted baluster forms were stretched, squashed, and added to in a multitude of combinations. Feet were stepped, domed, and flattened, and bowl forms were equally varied *(Figure 5)*. Much of this playing with the medium had its parallels in sixteenth-century Venice, but now the bowl shapes were being developed for specific purposes—for champagne, cordials, ale, syllabub, and so forth.

About 1710 entire stems began to be shaped in molds, in contrast to the earlier use of molded stem elements and, of course, molded feet such as that of the magnificent Clay Bank stem *(Figure 2)*. The molded stems were at first four-sided but soon developed more, while the shoulders were decorated with molded diamonds, stars, or sometimes

FIGURE 5

Stems with baluster and balustroid variations: (1) true baluster containing a tear beneath a flattened knop and collar; about 1705–1720. (2) inverted baluster with a knop at its junction with the foot, a tear extends through both baluster and knop; about 1710–1725. (3) a hollow drop knop over a flattened knop and beneath a collar separating it from the thistle-shaped bowl; about 1710–1725. (4) straight stem with a central, angular knop and a flattened knop at the junction of stem and foot, the bowl waisted; about 1715–1735. (5) solid balustroid stem with multiple knops, the bowl bucket-shaped; about 1740–1755.

FIGURE 6

A pair of inverted-baluster stemmed wine glasses found together near John Coke's tavern (Coke-Garrett House) amid a large quantity of refuse discarded in the period 1750–1760. The glasses have folded feet, inverted baluster stems containing large tears, knops at the junctions of feet and stems, and waisted bowls containing small tears in their thick bases. Such glasses are usually dated around 1710, but it seems likely that their true range is within the period 1715–1740.

FIGURE 7

Silesian or pedestal-stemmed wine glass from the John Custis well into which it was thrown about 1759. The glass has a rare molded domed foot with radial ribbing and diamond-shaped bosses, a form similar to that often seen on sweetmeat glasses of the second decade of the eighteenth century. The hexagonally molded stem contains a torpedo-shaped tear, and is decorated on alternate shoulders with diamond-shaped bosses. The round-funnel bowl is separated from the stem by a pad or neck, and contains a small tear in its thick base. This important glass was probably made in the period 1719–1730.

FIGURE 8

Wine glasses with stems drawn out from trumpet or waisted bowls. With the possible exception of No. 1, which might date as early as 1720, these are typical tavern glasses of the second quarter and middle of the eighteenth century. The stems of Nos. 1 and 2 contain elongated tears, while the others have small, round tears in their thick bowl bases. Nos. 1 and 2 have plain trumpet bowls; the others are waisted. No. 2 has an unusually small, yet heavy, folded foot; No. 3 has a plain foot; that of No. 4 is light and delicately folded.

with crowns. These last were often associated with relief inscriptions on the stem sides lauding the coronation of George I (1714). Two splendid examples of these so-called Silesian stems were found in an abandoned well shaft on the home site of John Custis and are thought to have been thrown out by his erstwhile daughter-in-law, Martha Washington, when she stripped the house in 1759 *(Figures 1 and 7)*. One of these glasses also possesses a cast foot with embossed diamonds similar to those used on the shoulders of other glasses of this type.

Although molded stems continued to be made at least until the mid-eighteenth century, they were never common, perhaps indicating a lack of popular acceptance of the austerity of straight lines in an essentially plastic medium. Much more widely used were glasses whose stems were decorated with hollow internal channels twisted into corkscrews and multiple spirals. These "air-twist" stems may have developed as early as 1725, although they did not become common for another fifteen years *(Figure 9)*. At first the twists themselves were considered to be sufficient ornament and the stems were therefore straight, but by 1750 the novelty had worn off and glassmakers were shaping the stems

FIGURE 9
Air-twist stems, typical of the more decorative tavern glasses of the period 1735–1750. All three have plain feet. Nos. 1 and 2 have trumpet bowls, their stems decorated with nine- and eight-ply spirals respectively. No. 3 has a two-ply corkscrew within the stem, and probably had an ogee bowl.

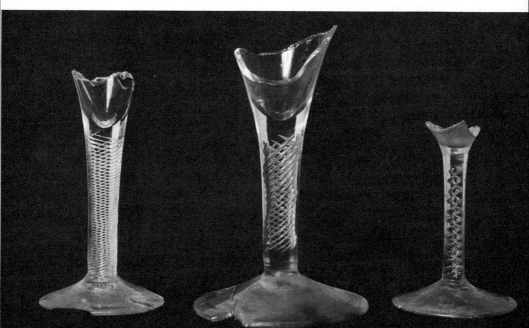

into knopped and balustroid excesses *(Figure 10),* some of them extremely attractive but others simply fussy. Air-twist glasses were described in the eighteenth century as "worm'd," and advertisements for them occurred in two Boston newspapers in 1746.

At the same time that air-twists were losing favor, another innovation was emerging, that of decorating the interior of the stems with opaque glass rods or ribbons which could be similarly twisted. Here the technique involved mounting the white glass rods in a mold and pouring the clear metal around them. In addition to simple spirals and corkscrews, many different and delicate patterns were devised by using rods of different sizes and twisting them in different directions. The result is generally classified as an "enamel-twist" and first appeared around 1750 *(Figures 12 and 13).* However, it was in reality not in the least novel, being a revival and adaptation of the *millefiori* technique developed in Roman Alexandria, and of the white *latticinio* ornament popular in Venice and among the *façon de Venise* glassmakers of the

FIGURE 10
Baluster and knopped air-twist stems of the mid-eighteenth century. No. 1 and No. 2 are decorated with eight-ply spirals and No. 3 with a ten-ply. Nos. 2 and 3 are types that often had waisted bowls and were sometimes engraved with Jacobite symbols.

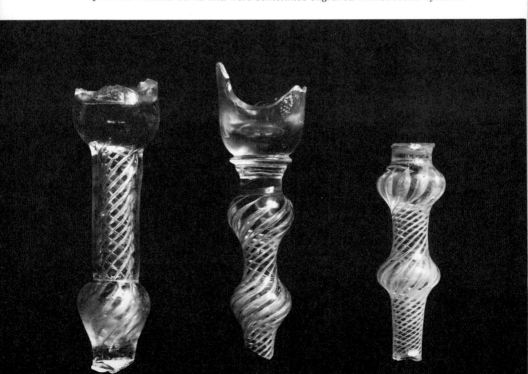

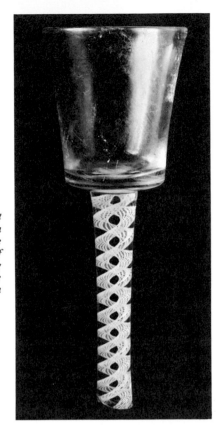

FIGURE 11
Wine glass with bucket bowl and a straight opaque-white twist stem decorated with a pair of spiral gauzes. Glasses of this type are found wheel-engraved with pictures of privateers that operated out of Bristol during the Seven Years' War (1756–1763.) The Williamsburg glass almost certainly had a plain foot.

FIGURE 12
Straight stems with opaque-white twists in various styles. No. 1 is decorated with a pair of spiral tapes within a single multi-ply spiral band. No. 2 has a spiral gauze within a single narrow spiral band. No. 3 has an outlined lace twist. All three glasses have plain feet. No. 1 had a plain trumpet bowl, No. 2 a short, round funnel bowl, and No. 3 a rib-molded ogee bowl. All date from the third quarter of the eighteenth century.

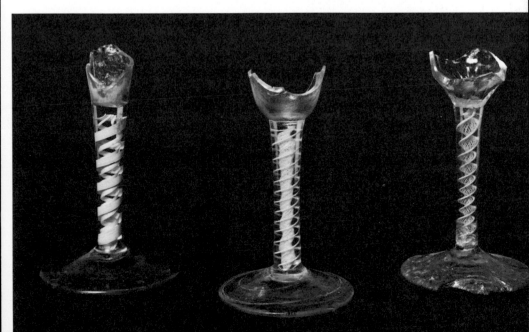

Netherlands in the sixteenth century. By 1765 the enamel-twists needed a new development if they were to retain their popularity, and so colored rods were added to or substituted for the plain white. While opaque-twists are relatively common in Williamsburg in contexts of the third quarter of the eighteenth century, colored-twists are rare, although a few examples in red, green, and blue have been found.

A new style-setting consideration arose in 1745/46 when the Glass Excise Act was passed taxing glass by weight. This prompted the makers to lighten their balusters and to seek more ways of decorating less glass. The solution was found outside the factories, in the shops of cutters and engravers. English lead glass was eminently suited to the cutter's wheel, a technique developed to dramatic perfection in Germany by the beginning of the eighteenth century and brought to England by German craftsmen in the reign of George I. However, the early efforts to apply cutting to existing English baluster stem designs were sometimes disastrous, transforming graceful curves into a multitude of disagreeable angles. Not until glasses were designed to take advantage of the reflective quality of cut facets did something new and exciting begin to be achieved.

It has been argued that instead of encouraging the use of cutting, the 1745 Excise Act was a deterrent, causing glasses to become thinner and more slender and thus less suited to the cutter's wheel. The alternative view holds that whereas the earlier weighty knops and balusters were not designed to be cut, later straight stems—which used less glass but were basically uninteresting—were enhanced by cutting. Archaeological evidence supports the latter view in that examples of English cut glass before 1750 are extremely rare, while specimens dating in the period 1750–1770 are more common. The majority of examples of cutting found in Williamsburg occur on straight stems *(Figure 13, left)*, occasionally with central cusps and adorned with hexagonal or diamond-shaped facets. Nearly all can be dated between the years 1755 and 1785, with the strong probability that they were in Williamsburg before 1776.

Wheel engraving, like cutting, was a German art that had reached peaks of technical brilliance by the beginning of the eighteenth century, and it was brought to England by German and Dutch craftsmen who eventually taught it to English workmen, although with results that must often have been the despair of the tutors.

The decorative designs fell into four main classes: armorial and inscriptive; pictorial; foliate and floral; and formal, with swags, bands, and hatching *(Figure 13, center).* The first group, those with heraldic

FIGURE 13
Wine glasses plain and fancy. No. 1 has a straight stem decorated with wheel-cut hexagonal facets, a plain foot, and a tapered round-funnel bowl; about 1760–1770. No. 2 has a straight stem, plain foot, and an ogee bowl decorated with simple wheel-engraving in a hatched swag pattern at the rim; about 1765–1780. No. 3 is undecorated, has a plain foot, a straight stem drawn out from a tapered round-funnel bowl, and dates from the last quarter of the eighteenth century.

devices or with personal or patriotic inscriptions, generally date within the period 1690–1740. They are rare and none has been found in Williamsburg excavations. The pictorial group, comprising ships and hunting and pastoral scenes, began in the late 1730s and continued into the nineteenth century, the earliest competing with the older and infinitely more delicate work of diamond-point engravers. No pictorial examples have yet been found in Williamsburg, but fragments of a mid-eighteenth-century tumbler or beaker bearing a skillfully executed ship have been excavated at Lee Hall (the original Lee family home site) in Virginia.

The English engravers, never able to match the formal baroque splendor of the Nuremberg and Augsburg products, developed their own floral and foliate motifs. The best known was the heraldic rose and

FIGURE 14

Tumblers of various sizes and shapes. No. 1 slightly flaring above the waist, No. 2 rather similar but less waisted, No. 3 barrel-shaped. Tumblers are difficult to date with accuracy, but these come from archaeological contexts of about 1765–1770, 1770–1775, and 1782–1790, respectively.

two buds associated with the 1745 Jacobite Rebellion and emblematic of the Old Pretender "James III" and his sons, Henry and Charles Edward Stuart. Not all rose-engraved glasses, however, are evidence of secret rebel sympathies. Others were decorated with forget-me-nots and thistles (again with Jacobite associations); ale glasses were adorned with hops and ears of barley, cider glasses with apples, boughs, or apple trees; wine glasses carried vine leaves and bunches of grapes, and others, apropos of nothing, sported daffodils or flowers of indeterminate parentage. It is evident from contemporary newspaper advertisements that considerable numbers of these "flower'd" glasses reached America. On June 8, 1761, Lewis Deblois announced in the *Boston Gazette* that he could provide his customers with "Hogsheads best engrav'd flower'd wine glasses and decanters." On July 6, the same newspaper carried an advertisement inserted by one William Maxwell offering "Wine-Glasses of the newest engrav'd and cutt-fashion." Later, on November 26, 1764, the *Boston Gazette* carried Mary Gallop's advertisement stating that she had "for Sale Flower'd Decanters, Wine Glasses, Cruets, Glass Salvers of all sizes."

The best preserved item of wheel-engraved glass recovered from Williamsburg excavations was found in the well at Wetherburn's Tavern, a small so-called one shot decanter decorated with grapes, vine leaves, flowers, and a cartouche inscribed MADEIRA *(Figure 15).* The style was known as a label decanter and was popular in the third quarter of the eighteenth century. An advertiser in the English *Norwich Mercury* for December 26, 1755, offered "new fashioned decanters with inscriptions engraven on them, Port, Claret, Mountain, etc., etc." Nine years later a New York storekeeper advertised in the *New York Gazette, or Weekly Post-Boy* that he could provide "new fashioned decanters labelled Madeira."

One of the most difficult questions to answer is: How new fashioned was "new fashioned" glassware when it was thus advertised in the colonial newspapers? Were the styles really hot off the iron or were they simply new to America? Archaeological evidence suggests that glass shapes continued in use in Williamsburg for a good many years after the styles (according to most glass specialists) had ceased being

FIGURE 15
Miniature label decanter engraved MADEIRA; about 1760. This is the best preserved example of wheel-engraving yet recovered from Williamsburg excavations.

FIGURE 16
Mushroom-knopped stem and gadrooned bowl fragment from an elegant rummer or mead glass. Although of a class usually attributed to about 1690, this example is thought to be a revival attributable to the 1740s.

made in England. There are a number of possible explanations: First, that the glass of the early eighteenth century was heavy and strong and therefore likely to have had a long life; second, that there may have been an appreciable lag between the time that styles became popular in England and their finding favor in America; third, that English glass sellers deliberately unloaded obsolete types onto their less discerning colonial customers; fourth, that English glassmakers continued to make shapes for export that they no longer produced for home consumption; and fifth, that the glass specialists are sometimes too narrow in their dating of the surviving pieces.

There may be grains of truth in all these arguments, but one fact is inescapable: Glasses of types that theoretically should have been made in the first years of the eighteenth century often turn up in contexts dating from its third quarter. As these anomalies are not confined to home sites but also occur around taverns, it is difficult to contend that the glasses, being fragile, had been treated with special care. Appearances can sometimes be deceiving, however, as is demonstrated by a fragmentary rummer discarded at Wetherburn's Tavern about 1755 *(Figure 16)*. The gadrooned bowl is comparable to those of several well-known English glasses made around 1690, but the style was briefly revived in the 1740s for what are often described as mead glasses. When first found, this example was attributed to the end of the seventeenth century, but the later date now seems more likely.

The survival of early types into late Williamsburg contexts might be used to support the argument that Virginia taste in glass was somewhat conservative. Like all such contentions, this one should be treated with caution. Nevertheless it would appear, at least from comparing contemporary newspaper advertisements with excavated glassware, that homes in the larger northern cities, such as New York and Boston, contained a greater variety of ornamental drinking glasses, decanters, cruets, salts, and the like, than did those of Williamsburg. A typical New York advertisement read as follows:

> George Ball, who has removed into Carman-street, next door to Alderman Gautier, has received by the last London and Bristol Vessels, a general assortment of glass ware, consisting of flower'd

and cut pint, half, and quarter pint tumblers; plain pint, half and
quarter pint tumblers; flower'd and cut pint and quart decanters;
a variety of neat enamel'd cut wine glasses, chamber lamps, bird
glasses and salt linings, etc. with an assortment of cheap glass fit
for the country.[2]

Very few pieces of colored glass have been found in Williamsburg
excavations in contexts dating before the Revolution, and most of the
pieces from later deposits are probably of American manufacture. Although the better English glassmakers had produced decorative metal
in green, blue, and purple as early as the seventeenth century, they
made little or no use of it through the first half of the eighteenth century.
In the second half of that century colored metals were used at glasshouses in London, Birmingham, Stourbridge, Newcastle, and Bristol.
The last was best known for its rich blue glass, the production of which
is believed to have begun around 1763 using a supply of fine cobalt
(smalt) from Saxony. Bristol was not alone in its production of blue
metal, and various factories used it for decanters, cruet and smelling
bottles, liners for salts, pickle stands, and other decorative items.

The first recorded manufacturer of colored glass in America was
Henry William Stiegel at whose factory at Manheim, Pennsylvania, it
was made between 1769 and 1774. The products ranged from pocket
flasks to jars for flowers, many of the pieces pattern-molded and
fashioned from blue, green, or amethyst metals. Unfortunately it is
generally impossible to be certain that a piece is Stiegel's and not an
English or continental European product. The same is true of Stiegel's
enameled glass beakers and bottles, which are often indistinguishable
from the products of Bohemia or the northern Netherlands *(Figure 18)*.

A few fragments of octagonal bottles (originally with threaded
pewter collars and screw caps) decorated with foliate designs in blue,
white, yellow, and red enamel, have been found in Williamsburg
excavations, as also have fragments of tumblers decorated with a comparable pallet but uncertain design. One small fragment from Wetherburn's Tavern had first been wheel engraved, suggesting that its

---

2. New York *Gazette and the Weekly Mercury*, April 15, 1771.

enameling was a later addition. The quality of the enameling is generally poor and "peasant" in character. It bears little resemblance to the remarkable armorial and rococo work done by William and Mary Beilby in the early 1760s at Newcastle-on-Tyne and now so prized by collectors of English glass; nor, for that matter, are the excavated fragments in the same class as the enameled opaque-white products of Bristol in the third quarter of the century.

Opaque-white—derived from the inclusion of tin oxide in the mix—

FIGURE 17   FIGURE 18

FIGURE 17
Left: *The remains of a rare and heavy lead-glass mug or jug with a massive strapped handle, the body decorated on the shoulder with a single trail; about 1710–1745.* Right: *Cruet bottle with lip missing and only the handle terminals surviving; first half of eighteenth century.*

FIGURE 18
Pewter capped flask, soda metal, decorated in enamel colors, probably made in Bohemia or the Netherlands about 1770. This example is in Colonial Williamsburg's Department of Collections, but the type is comparable to fragments found at Wetherburn's Tavern and on other Williamsburg archaeological sites.

FIGURE 19
The only more-or-less-intact item of opaque-white glass from Williamsburg. This drinking mug may have been made at Bristol about 1765; it was found in excavations near Anthony Hay's Cabinetmaking Shop.

was a Bristol speciality that began around 1750. It was also made elsewhere in England, notably at Birmingham, but the latter metals were less opaque, more closely resembling the contemporary *Milchglas* from Germany. There is no knowing how much opaque-white glass was imported into America in the quarter-century preceding the Revolution. The usually helpful newspaper advertisements can be misleading in that they frequently listed "White or Green Glass" or "white and green Bottles." They were not referring to white as a color but using the word to describe a clear or colorless metal, the term dating back at least to the 1670s. Even more confusing and potentially misleading was the appearance in the mid-eighteenth century of the term "White Flint," so misleading in fact that one of the most distinguished of glass authorities has taken it to be synonymous with opaque-white.

    In 1736 a Bristol glassmaker, Humphrey Perrott, obtained a patent for a new and hotter melting furnace that imparted an added brilliance and clarity to his metal. When he died in 1752, Perrott was described as being the "proprietor of the White Flint Glasshouse at Bedminster," and it is supposed that he coined the new term "White Flint" to describe his improved wares. By the end of the eighteenth century there were several "white or flint glass houses" in the Bristol area. By 1775 "white flint Glass" was sufficiently common for a New York newspaper[3] to carry an advertisement offering a penny a pound for it when broken, leaving no doubt that the term meant something other than opaque-white.[4]

Fragments from two or three opaque-white vessels (usually pitchers, mugs, or bowls) are recovered from most Williamsburg sites, a relatively small number compared to the hundreds of clear-metal glasses and vessels represented on those same sites. The most complete opaque-white specimen yet recovered in Williamsburg is a mug or can *(Figure 19),* probably broken about 1770, that was found beside Anthony Hay's Cabinetmaking Shop.

Wine bottles and glasses were undoubtedly the most common glass vessel forms of the seventeenth and eighteenth centuries. Glass, however, was an extraordinarily adaptable material and an enormous variety of objects could be made from it, as we are reminded by the diversity of fragments recovered from Williamsburg excavations. They include pieces from candlesticks, sconces, chandeliers, salvers, sugar crushers, linen smoothers, apothecaries' pestles, funnels, urinals, lamps, ink wells, marbles, and bird cage bottles. As a rule such items are represented by single fragments too small to be recognized by anyone but a specialist in the field. An exception is provided by the bird bottle *(Figure 20)* found in an abandoned cellar on Nicholson Street not far from the Hay Cabinetmaking Shop. This distinctive vessel, with its anthropomorphic finial, seems to have been popular from about 1720 on through the eighteenth century. Such items were sold in Williamsburg as "bird glasses" in 1766, and an example attached to its cage may be seen in Thomas Rowlandson's engraving "The Tax Gatherer," published in 1799.

---

3. New York *Journal or the General Advertiser,* August 3, 1775.
4. The term "flint white" was also used to describe English white salt-glazed stoneware.

Although bottles for birds are represented in the Williamsburg archaeological collections by a single specimen, bottles for people are there by the thousand. Indeed, broken glass wine bottles have provided approximately half the artifacts recovered from the soil of Williamsburg. Eleven hundred were found in a single basement under the present United States Post Office, a basement abandoned and filled with trash about 1770 *(Figure 21)*. The term "wine bottle" is used rather loosely to describe all bottles that were on occasion employed for that purpose. The same shapes were used for beer, ale, spirits, whale oil, paint, and fruit: one found in Williamsburg contained bird shot. It was not until the nineteenth century that bottles began to be made with shapes peculiar to certain types of wine, such as Champagne, Bordeaux, and Moselle. Nevertheless, many collectors, and some museums, erroneously refer to the cylindrical bottles of the 1730s onward as rum bottles, while they call all square sectioned specimens Dutch gin bottles—regardless of whether they were made in England or on the continent, or whether they are known to have held gin.

FIGURE 20
Left: *An ornamental lead glass bird feeder or fountain with a tricorn-hatted, anthropo-morphic finial. The hopper is missing. This example was found in London.* Right: *The finial, base; and hopper from a feeder of similar type found in Williamsburg. The style seems to have been used for bird cages throughout most of the eighteenth century.*

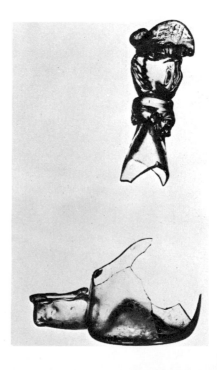

The earliest wine bottles were shaped in four-sided molds and were frequently sealed with threaded pewter caps. They are often found on archaeological sites dating before the last quarter of the seventeenth century, but are rarely discovered intact because their flat walls and sharp corners made them very fragile. The example illustrated in *Figure 22* was found by Williamsburg archaeologists at Denbigh plantation in Warwick County. By 1650, and perhaps a few years earlier, a new bottle shape had been devised, one that relied less on molding and was infinitely stronger, but whose long neck and small base area made it difficult to store and easy to overturn. The illustrated example *(Figure 23)* was found in London but was made for Ralph Wormeley of Jamestown who died in 1651; it is the earliest documented bottle of its type. This general shape persisted for about twenty years, by the end of which time necks were being shortened and the bodies made more angular. The example shown in *Figure 24* dates around 1680 and is the earliest found in Williamsburg. By 1700 the shape had changed again, the body sagging down on itself and the base spreading, a profile ungallantly known by some collectors as the "Queen Anne shape" *(Figure 25)*. Stable though such bottles were, they were still difficult to pack and store; these factors, coupled with a desire to house bottled

FIGURE 21
Wine bottle fragments from a single Williamsburg cellar being sorted and classified in the archaeological laboratory.

wine inverted or on its side (keeping the corks constantly moist), prompted the next evolutionary step, one well illustrated by *Figure 26,* a bottle made for Samuel Cobbs of Williamsburg and thrown away around 1735. Here the body has become taller and straighter sided, a trend that continued through the eighteenth century. By the time of the Revolution the wine bottle reached pretty much the shape that it retains to this day *(Figure 35),* the principal difference being that it is now entirely mold-and-machine made.

FIGURE 22
A square-bodied bottle with the remains of a threaded pewter collar and cap attached to the lip, a type common in Virginia in the second quarter of the seventeenth century. This fine example was found in excavations at Denbigh plantation near Newport News; about 1640.

FIGURE 23
A wine bottle made for Ralph Wormeley of Jamestown who died in 1651. This example, one of two found in London, is the earliest documented specimen of its type yet discovered. A seal from the same matrix was found on Wormeley's home site at Jamestown.

FIGURE 22   FIGURE 23

The vast majority of mid- to late eighteenth-century wine bottles were cylindrical, although a few found on Williamsburg sites are wider at the shoulder than at the base, giving them a body shape akin to that of a flowerpot. Such bottles are French. Others, whose origin has not been satisfactorily pinned down, were shaped in octagonal molds, and the majority that have been found in Williamsburg bear the seal of merchant John Greenhow and the date 1770 *(Figure 27)*. Another bottle having a Greenhow seal but dated 1769 is thought to have been found at Surry Court House *(Figure 28);* this, too, was octagonally molded but of different proportions. It seems likely that Greenhow purchased both types from a factory specializing in these angular shapes. As the molding technique was uncommon in England at that date, it is tempting to seek some other place of origin, perhaps in this country.

Bottles adorned with identifying and dated seals were in use as early as about 1650, but the earliest dated example yet recorded from Virginia

FIGURE 24
The earliest glass wine bottle found in Williamsburg, a shape common in the period 1685–1700.

FIGURE 25
A bottle typical of the first twenty years of the eighteenth century. This example with its cork intact and retaining some of its wine contents was found in the well at Bassett Hall.

FIGURE 24

FIGURE 25

| FIGURE 26 | FIGURE 27 | FIGURE 28 |

FIGURE 26
A bottle bearing the seal of Samuel Cobbs and found on his Williamsburg lot. Since Cobbs left the city in 1735, it is reasonable to date this bottle within the years 1730–1735.

FIGURE 27
An octagonally molded bottle (all sides of equal width) made for merchant John Greenhow of Williamsburg and dated 1770.

FIGURE 28
An octagonally molded bottle made for John Greenhow of Williamsburg and dated 1769, the metal amber in color.

was found by Colonial Williamsburg archaeologists working at Tutter's Neck in James City County. The bottle, marked "Richard Burbydge 1701," was found in a rubbish pit along with others bearing the initials of the plantation owner, Frederick Jones *(Figure 29)*. The earliest dated bottle found in Williamsburg itself (and the second earliest from the state) was discovered near the home of John Custis, father-in-law of

FIGURE 29

FIGURE 29
Two of more than a hundred broken bottles found in a rubbish pit at Tutter's Neck in James City County. Left: *One of five examples bearing the initials of Frederick Jones who lived on the plantation site between 1702 and 1708.* Right: *The earliest dated bottle yet found in Virginia. It was made for Richard Burbydge of James City County and is dated 1701.*

FIGURE 30
A bottle bearing the seal IOHN CUSTIS 1713, found in a well on his home site in Williamsburg.

FIGURE 30

Martha Dandridge Custis Washington; it bears his name and the date 1713 *(Figure 30)*. More than sixty broken examples were recovered from the site, most of them from the well.

Relatively few seventeenth- and eighteenth-century wine bottles were marked with seals, and of those that were, perhaps one in twenty was dated. However, because of the enormous number of broken bottles found in Williamsburg excavations, seals are well represented in the archaeological collections. Among the prominent Virginians thus

FIGURE 31

Some bottle seals found in Williamsburg excavations: (1) perhaps Francis Nicholson, governor of Virginia, 1698–1705. (2) John Blair, 1731, a prominent Williamsburg merchant. (3) John Custis, a plantation owner and Williamsburg resident, the seal dating about 1730. (4) Thomas Dansi, 1739, a ship's captain and landowner of King William and Spotsylvania counties. (5) arms of the first Earl Poulett, who became a Knight of the Garter in 1712 and died in 1743. (6) John Tazewell, 1768, a Williamsburg lawyer. (7) William Prentis, a Williamsburg merchant who died in 1765. (8) George Wythe, 1768, first professor of law at the College of William and Mary, and a signer of the Declaration of Independence. (9) Thomas Hornsby, 1769, a Williamsburg merchant and tailor who died in 1772. (10) Benjamin Powell, 1774, a Williamsburg wheelwright and builder who died after 1789.

recalled are George Wythe, John Blair, John Tazewell, John and William Prentis, builder Benjamin Powell, and a ship's captain named Thomas Dansi *(Figure 31).* From other Virginia excavations have come the seals of Carter Braxton, Mann Page II, John Washington, Henry Lee, Robert Carter, George Mason, Richard Eppes, and Richard Randolph.

The so-called wine bottles of the colonial period were not only to be found in homes and taverns, they were also used by apothecaries, and one of the largest assemblages from a single Williamsburg site came from property owned by Dr. George Gilmer in the mid-eighteenth century. Some indication of the variety of his stock is indicated by an advertisement in the *Virginia Gazette* for June 20, 1745:

Just imported in the Ship Neptune,
Capt. Crawford, *from LONDON*

FIGURE 32
A snuff or blacking bottle typical of the third quarter of the eighteenth century. This undamaged example was found in a well near the James Geddy House.

A Large Quantity of Medicines and Druggs, with *Annodyne* Neclaces, Barleys, Cloves, Mace, Nutmegs, Cinnamon, Sweet Oil, Barber's ditto, Oil of Behn, Prunes, Sago, *Stoughton's* Elixir, *Squire's* and *Daffy's* Elixirs, *Bateman's* Drops, *Lockyer's* and *Anderson's* Pills, Oil-cloth, *Scotch* Snuff, Goldleaf, and *Dutch* Metal, Tamerinds, candy'd Ginger and Eryngo, Smelling-bottles, *Hungary* Water, *Spaw* and *Pyrmont* Waters, &c.

The Scotch snuff was probably sold in bottles similar to that shown in *Figure 32*, a type generally used either for snuff or blacking. The spa waters were usually bottled in their place of origin, but in bottles frequently bearing seals with English inscriptions. Examples of the Pyrmont water seals were found on the Gilmer property, those dating from the mid-eighteenth century being adorned with the arms of Waldeck and marked PYRMONT WATER. Bottles from that spa exported earlier in the century had been marked with a smaller seal embossed PIERMONT WATER around a star. The Pyrmont bottles closely resembled the angular French shape mentioned on page 35. While a few of those marked Piermont are of that shape, the majority would seem to have been more akin to the squat English bottles of the first quarter of the eighteenth century, but differing in that the necks were generally taller and had very roughly applied string rims, unlike the neat V-tooling of those on English specimens. The same tool that was used to apply the Piermont Water seal was often used to press the trailed string rim to the neck, and in doing so impressed part of the seal onto it *(Figure 33)*.

Somewhat akin to the snuff bottles—in that they had wide mouths—were bottles designed for storing fruit or slow-pouring semi-liquids. Three intact examples were found together in excavations at Wetherburn's Tavern, one of them resembling a long-necked snuff bottle and the others a hitherto unrecorded version of the squat wine bottle of the early eighteenth century *(Figure 34)*. They are thought to have contained cherry brandy or brandied cherries that had been buried to mature about 1750. Two later varieties of wide-mouthed bottles, shown in *Figure 35*, were found at Anthony Hay's Cabinetmaking Shop site in a context of about 1770. The ordinary wine bottles found with them clearly show how the body shapes remained the same while the necks and mouths were adapted to receive the bulky contents.

FIGURE 33
Piermont and Pyrmont Water bottle seals and, at right, the neck of a Piermont Water bottle whose string rim has been pressed to it by using the same tool that was employed to stamp the seal.

FIGURE 34
Wide-mouthed bottles for bottling fruit, the center example with a hexagonally molded body. These rare examples had been buried together behind Wetherburn's Tavern about 1750.

FIGURE 35
A group of conventional and wide-necked bottles found together near the site of Anthony Hay's Cabinetmaking Shop. The group was buried in the period 1770–1780.

FIGURE 36
Green pharmaceutical phials from various Williamsburg sites. These shapes were common in the first half of the eighteenth century.

Small medicine bottles or phials belong to a class of their own, being fashioned from a pale or blue-green metal of a quality superior to that used for wine bottles. However, it was common for both to be made in the same glasshouses. In the late sixteenth and early seventeenth centuries pharmaceutical bottles were made in a great variety of shapes, many of them molded, and colors ranged from a pale straw through deep amber to a rich emerald green. By the mid-seventeenth century, however, a uniformity of color and shape had developed, the phials being olive green and essentially cylindrical but with such weak shoulders that some were actually conical. These so-called steeple bottles have often been thought to be much older than they actually are. By the end of the seventeenth century, shoulders had become more angular and the walls vertical, although rims often continued to be broad and flat, a characteristic of the earlier weak-shouldered forms *(Figure 36)*. Most of these bottles were of a more or less uniform green, although there were other colors, notably a group of pale blue bottles resembling miniature wine bottles of the late seventeenth century, a style that continued (with narrower string rims) into the first half of the eighteenth century.

42

FIGURE 37   FIGURE 38

FIGURE 37
Clear or "white" metal phials thrown down Wetherburn's Tavern well about 1770. The standing example is still corked and waxed, and retains part of its original contents.

FIGURE 38
A cello-shaped bottle for Robert Turlington's Balsam of Life, the bottle dated March 26, 1750. This seemingly unrecorded type was found in an abandoned well shaft near Wetherburn's Tavern.

By the mid-eighteenth century, medicine bottles were being produced in a clear, lead metal. Some were merely slightly elongated copies of the green pharmaceutical phials *(Figure 37),* but others were mold-made and were embossed with the name of the patentee or purveyor of specific elixirs. The best known of those was Turlington's balsam, a multi-ingredient cure-all first patented in 1744. By 1750 Robert Turlington was dispensing his balsam in proprietary bottles, the only recorded and more or less intact example of which was found in a well shaft at Wetherburn's Tavern in Williamsburg *(Figure 38).* Distinctive though the bottle was, it did not prevent competitors from pirating Mr. Turlington's balsam, and in 1754 he changed the shape, at the same time condemning those "Persons who buying up my empty bottles, have basely and wickedly put therein a vile, spurious Counterfeit-Sort."

The new bottle bore the date "JANUY 26, 1754." Unfortunately neither Mr. Turlington's complaint nor his new bottles put an end to the counterfeiting, and American versions of the bottle (the later ones usually in a pale blue metal) were produced well into the nineteenth century. There were even counterfeits of counterfeits that resulted in changes to the lettering (e.g. BALSOM and BALSLM) and to the date, January 26th moving to the 28th. According to a broadsheet published in the period 1755–57 and now in the collection of the Pennsylvania Historical Society, the correct legend should read as follows:

BY THE KINGS ROYALL PATENT GRANTED TO
ROBT. TURLINGTON FOR HIS INVENTED BALSAM OF LIFE
LONDON
JANUY 26, 1754

It is reasonable to conclude that any variations are either contemporary or later copies, and, as *Figure 39* shows, Colonial Williamsburg's collections include three such counterfeits.

FIGURE 39

Pirated copies of Robert Turlington's 1754 bottle. The example on the left was found near the site of the Printing Office and is probably contemporary with Turlington's own bottles. The others were found in a well at the Wythe House, where they had been discarded after 1853. The example on the right is pale blue in color and is the most recent, probably dating no earlier than 1820.

Although, as Dr. Gilmer's advertisement demonstrated, a considerable variety of patent medicines were sold and used in eighteenth-century Williamsburg, only the bottles for Turlington's Balsam have been found. Nevertheless, the documentary sources leave no doubt that other proprietary bottles were in use. In 1753 the Williamsburg apothecary Dr. James Carter wrote to England ordering "3 Quire Stoughton's Directions" and "½ Groce Stoughton Vials," clearly indicating that he intended to mix his own version of "Stoughton's Elixir." It is to be hoped that an example of this bottle will eventually be recovered from Williamsburg excavations. Fortunately, many sites are still to be explored, and there is every chance that much more glass will be recovered, some of which will almost certainly fill gaps both in our knowledge and in Colonial Williamsburg's archaeological collections.

FIGURE 40

American-made bottles of the first half of the eighteenth century. The snuff or blacking bottles at left and center are olive-amber and amber in color, while that at the right is a deep green. All three were found in a well beside the Wythe House where they had been thrown no earlier than 1853.

Figure*	*Colonial Williamsburg catalog number*	*Measurements*
1, No. 1.	3922. E.R.850X—4.B.	Ht. 5¼"
2.	3923. E.R.850X—4.B.	Ht. 6¼"
3.	3924. E.R.850X—4.B.	Ht. 6¾"
4.	3925. E.R.850X—4.B.	Ht. 5⅜"
5.	3926. E.R.850X—4.B.	Ht. 6⅞"
2a.	Smithsonian Institution	Ht. 5¼"
3, No. 1.	3927—9.L.	Ht. 2½"
2.	3928—18.C.	Ht. 3"
3.	3929—2.J.4.	Ht. 2½"
4, No. 1.	3933—9.L.	Ht. 4½"
2.	3934—2.B.1.	Ht. 3¾"
3.	3935—17.B.1.	Ht. 4½"
4.	3936—17.D.5.	Ht. 4½"
5.	3937—18.E.	Ht. 4½"
5, No. 1.	3938.E.R.140—27.B.	Ht. 3½"
2.	3939—9.L.	Ht. 3½"
3.	3940.E.R.140—27.B.	Ht. 3¼"
4.	3941.E.R.748—28.D.	Ht. 5½"
5.	3942—9.L.	Ht. 4¾"
6, No. 1.	3930. E.R.157G—27.A.	Ht. 6⅜"
2.	3932. E.R.157G—27.A.	Ht. 6⅝"
7.	3943.E.R.850X—4.B.	Ht. 6"
8, No. 1.	3944—27.A.	Ht. 4½"
2.	3945. E.R.1011R—9.N.	Ht. 5¼"
3.	3946—29.H.2.	Ht. 6¼"
4.	3991. E.R.157G—27.A.	Ht. 5¾"
5.	3948. E.R.1268N—29.G.	Ht. 6½"
9, No. 1.	3949. E.R.247G—28.D.	Ht. 5⅜"
2.	3950. E.R. 247G—28.D.	Ht. 6¼"
3.	3951—2.B.1.	Ht. 4¼"
10, No. 1.	3952—17.J.	Ht. 3¾"
2.	3953—9.L.	Ht. 4"
3.	3954—30.C.	Ht. 3"
11.	3955—27.A.	Ht. 5¼"

* All numbering of multiple item illustrations is from left to right and from top to bottom row.

Figure	Colonial Williamsburg catalog number	Measurements
12, No. 1.	3956—O.C.	Ht. 4½″
2.	2086—28.F.4	Ht. 4½″
3.	3957. E.R.1114C—9P.	Ht. 4¾″
13, No. 1.	2087—28.F.4	Ht. 4⅞″
2.	3093. E.R.561—14.G.	Ht. 5⅜″
3.	3958. E.R.850V—4.B.	Ht. 4⅞″
14, No. 1.	3959. E.R.1340J—19.B.	Ht. 3⅞″
2.	3960. E.R.797D,G—4.B.	Ht. 6¼″
3.	3095. E.R. 532N—14.G.	Ht. 3⅝″
15.	3403. E.R.1135F—9.N.	Ht. 4″
16.	3961. E.R.1165G—9.N.	Ht. 3″
17, No. 1.	3962. E.R.987M—19.B.	Ht. 6½″
2.	3963—9.L.	Ht. 5⅝″
18.	1950—301	Ht. 6″
19.	3964. E.R.230D—28.D.	Ht. 6¼″
20, No. 1.	Guildhall Museum, London	Ht. 6⅛″
2.	2218—28.F.4	Ht. of upper frag. 3⅛″
22.	W.S.203	Ht. 10½″
23.	Noël Hume Collection	Ht. 8¼″
24.	3965—30.B.	Ht. 7¼″
	106—1.A.2.	Ht. 6¼″
26.	3966—O.C.	Ht. 7¾″
27.	125—28.F.4	Ht. 8¼″
28.	3944—O.C.	Ht. 11⅝″
29, No. 1.	Smithsonian Institution	Ht. 6¼″
2.	Smithsonian Institution	Ht. 6¼″
30.	3967. E.R.850X—4.B.	Ht. 7″
31, No. 1.	3968—16.A.1.	Diam. 1¼″
2.	3969—29.C.	Diam. 1⅜″
3.	3970—20.A.19.	Diam. 1⅜″
4.	3971. E.R.364B—28.D.	Diam. 1¾″

Figure	Colonial Williamsburg catalog number	Measurements
5.	3972. E.R.191—28.D.	Diam. 1½"
6.	3973—30.A.	Diam. 1⅞"
7.	3974—O.C.	Diam. 1¾"
8.	3975—20.A.19.	Diam. 1⅝"
9.	3976—Blk. 35.	Diam. 1⅜"
10.	3977—27.B.	Diam. 1⅜"
32.	3978. E.R.1340V—19.B.	Ht. 7⅛"
33, No. 1.	Upper seal 3979. E.R. 1268L—29.E.	Diam. 1 3/16"
2.	Lower seal 3980. E.R. 1268L—29.E.	Diam. 1⅝"
3.	Neck 163—29.A.2.	Ht. 4"
34, No. 1.	3980. E.R.1016C—9.N.	Ht. 5½"
2.	3981. E.R.1016C—9.N.	Ht. 8"
3.	3982. E.R.1016C—9.N.	Ht. 6"
35, No. 1.	5016. E.R.254C—28.D.	Ht. 8½"
2.	5017. E.R.254C—28.D.	Ht. 8⅜"
3.	5018. E.R.254C—28.D.	Ht. 7½"
4.	5019. E.R.254C—28.D.	Ht. 6¾"
5.	5020. E.R.254C—28.D.	Ht. 7¼"
6.	5021. E.R.254C—28.D.	Ht. 9"
7.	5022. E.R.254C—28.D.	Ht. 9¾"
36, No. 1.	3983. E.R.386—15.A.	Ht. 3¼"
2.	3988. E.R.1253—29.E.	Ht. 3¼"
3.	3984—2.H.4.	Ht. 2¾"
4.	3985. E.R.1268N—29.G.	Ht. 2⅛"
5.	790—29.G.	Ht. 2⅜"
6.	3986. E.R.1268N—29.G.	Ht. 2⅛"
7.	3987—17.E.	Ht. 6"
37, No. 1.	3763. E.R.1135F—9.N.	Ht. 3⅝"
2.	3990. E.R.1135F—9.N.	Ht. 3¼"
38.	3364. E.R.1139B—9.N.	Ht. 2⅞"
39, No. 1.	5023—18.H.	Ht. 2⅝"
2.	5034. E.R.44C—21.A.	Ht. 2½"
3.	5025. E.R.44C1—21.A.	Ht. 2½"
40, No. 1.	3991. E.R.44C8—21.A.	Ht. 4¼"
2.	3992. E.R.44C1—21.A.	Ht. 6"
3.	3992. E.R.44C9—21.A.	Ht. 4¾"